Original title:
A Heart Renewed

Author: Aron Pilviste
ISBN HARDBACK: 978-9916-89-814-7
ISBN PAPERBACK: 978-9916-89-815-4
ISBN EBOOK: 978-9916-89-816-1

Notes of New Beginnings

In the dawn's soft light, we're reborn,
Whispers of hope with each new morn.
Faith ignites a path so bright,
Guiding hearts towards the right.

Grace descends like gentle rain,
Washing away the weight of pain.
Each moment holds a sacred chance,
To rise anew, to dream, to dance.

Promises made, the spirit soars,
Opening wide, unclosing doors.
In prayer, we find our truest voice,
In silence, we learn to rejoice.

Love intertwines through every thread,
In unity, our worries shed.
With every breath, a hymn we sing,
A chorus of joy, it's awakening.

So let us walk, hand in hand,
Embracing futures, bright and grand.
In the heart's echo, a sacred song,
Together we're destined, where we belong.

The Bloom in the Broken

In the cracks where sorrow dwells,
Life dares to rise and swell.
A fragile petal, soft and bright,
Turns pain to beauty in the light.

From ashes, hope begins to wane,
Yet blooms may flourish in the rain.
A garden sprung from grit and strife,
God breathes the spirit back to life.

Waters of Renewal

In the depths of sacred streams,
Washes away our broken dreams.
Each drop a promise, pure and clear,
Brings forth the faith that conquers fear.

As ripples weave through barren clay,
New beginnings find their way.
The heart renewed, the soul reborn,
In God's embrace, the spirit's worn.

Shattered Chains

From shackles forged in silence deep,
We cry for freedom, faith to keep.
With every prayer, we break the night,
Into the dawn, we seek the light.

Forgive the past, let burdens fall,
With God’s strength, we rise and stand tall.
No chain can hold what love has freed,
In unity, we walk, we heed.

New Life

In winter's grip, where coldness grips,
A promise stirs, the spirit dips.
From seeds of grace in shadows laid,
Life bursts forth, unafraid.

With every breath, the angels sing,
Of new beginnings that love will bring.
Through trials faced, we come to find,
In every heart, a God aligned.

From Darkness to Divinity

Through valleys dark and paths unknown,
We seek the light; we are not alone.
With each step forward, dimmed by fears,
Faith shines brighter through the years.

From doubt's embrace, the soul takes flight,
Transcending shadows into light.
In grace, we find our destiny,
From darkness leads us to divinity.

Mending the Fractured Soul

In shadows deep, where hope had fled,
A whisper calls, its soft words spread.
The heart in pieces, torn and worn,
Yet grace descends, a new life born.

Through trials faced, our spirits rise,
The healing balm, a love so wise.
With every tear, a lesson learned,
In faith's embrace, the heart’s returned.

The hands of mercy gently hold,
A story bright, in faith retold.
Each fracture speaks of strength in plight,
The soul restored, a radiant light.

The Oasis of Mercy

In barren lands where thirst does reign,
A stream of grace flows through the pain.
The weary traveler finds a place,
To drink of love, to know His grace.

With every drop, a spirit stirs,
The heart renewed, as mercy purrs.
In kindness shared, our burdens fade,
An oasis found, where fears evade.

The gentle hands of peace bestow,
A tranquil heart, a path to grow.
In mercy's shade, we rise anew,
The breeze of hope, forever true.

The Lamp of Renewed Purpose

In darkness deep, the heart feels lost,
Yet shining bright, the light is tossed.
A lamp of faith that guides the way,
Illuminates the night to day.

With every flicker, courage blooms,
A sacred fire within consumes.
The path ahead, though steep and long,
In purpose found, we grow more strong.

As shadows flee and dawn breaks clear,
The whispers of our worth we hear.
In every step, His love ignites,
Our journey soars on wings of light.

Reflections of Divine Love

In quiet moments, still and pure,
A mirror held, our heart's allure.
Divine love spills, a sacred stream,
In every soul, a radiant dream.

Through trials faced, through joy and pain,
Reflections cast in love's refrain.
We see His face in every heart,
In every end, a brand new start.

In laughter shared and tears that flow,
The bonds of love continue to grow.
Each life a note in harmony,
In grace's song, we're truly free.

The Call of the Spirit

In the silence found within the heart,
Awakens a whisper, a sacred start.
Guided by the light, a gentle sway,
Leading the weary souls to pray.

With every breath, the spirit sings,
Echoing the peace that wisdom brings.
In moments of doubt, a presence near,
Calling us home, casting out fear.

In the depth of night, a star's soft gleam,
Illuminates the path, a holy dream.
Trust in this call, let your spirit soar,
Embrace the love, forevermore.

Illuminated Paths

Through the forest where shadows play,
A light emerges to guide the way.
With every step on the winding road,
We walk together, sharing the load.

The moonlight dances on leaves of grace,
As we seek the truth in a sacred space.
Voices of ages whisper and weave,
In this tapestry of hope, believe.

In moments of chaos, find a spark,
Illuminate the path through the dark.
Step by step, let love define,
Together we rise, your heart and mine.

The Color of Compassion

In every heart, a shade unfolds,
The hue of kindness, a warmth it holds.
With open arms and gentle eyes,
We paint the world with love that ties.

A tender touch can heal the soul,
Bridging the gaps, making us whole.
With every word, let kindness flow,
In the garden of life, watch compassion grow.

Through storms and trials, we stand tall,
The color of compassion, it conquers all.
In unity we flourish, hand in hand,
Together we rise, together we stand.

Fires of Transformation

From ashes rise the flames anew,
Burning brightly, a vibrant hue.
Through trials faced, a spirit forged,
In every struggle, our souls enlarged.

The fire ignites, it warms the night,
Leading us forth, into the light.
With every burn, the past released,
In the flames of change, find your peace.

Embrace the heat, let it embrace,
Transform the fears, with love replace.
In the dance of embers, find your way,
Fires of transformation, come what may.

Echoes of Divine Forgiveness

In shadows deep, where silence grows,
The whispered grace of mercy flows.
With open hearts, we seek the light,
In love's embrace, we find our might.

Forgive us, Lord, our fleeting ways,
Guide us through these earthly days.
In trials faced, we learn to stand,
With faith renewed, we clasp your hand.

As dawn breaks forth, new visions rise,
We share our burdens, hear our cries.
In unity, the spirit soars,
Together strong, our hope restores.

The past we leave, in you we're free,
In every heart, your tapestry.
With every step, your path we trace,
In your mercy, we find our place.

So let us walk, with joyful song,
In your forgiveness, we belong.
With echoes sweet, our souls align,
In love, O Lord, forever shine.

The Path of Renewal's Light

Amidst the trials, we seek your grace,
In every moment, we find our place.
The path ahead, though steep it seems,
Is brightened by our fervent dreams.

Renew our spirits, cleanse our hearts,
In every breath, your truth imparts.
With every dawn, a chance bestowed,
To walk with you upon this road.

Your light ignites our weary souls,
With every step, our purpose rolls.
Guided by faith, we rise anew,
In unity, we journey through.

With open eyes, we see the signs,
In nature's beauty, your love aligns.
The whispers soft, of peace divine,
In every heart, your love does shine.

So let us tread, with hope in hand,
For on this path, together we stand.
In renewal's grace, we find our sight,
United, we embrace your light.

Healing Waters of the Spirit

In stillness deep, the waters flow,
With healing touch, your blessings grow.
A sacred stream of love and care,
Our spirits rise, laid bare in prayer.

Wash over us, O gentle tide,
In every heart, you will abide.
The burdens lifted, peace restored,
In faith we trust, our soul's reward.

Each drop a promise, pure and bright,
In darkest hours, you are our light.
As flows the river, so flows our grace,
In every moment, your warm embrace.

The spirit sighs, in joyful gleam,
In healing waters, we dare to dream.
Beneath the surface, life anew,
In unity, we rise with you.

So let us drink from wells of love,
With grateful hearts, our souls will rise.
In healing waters, we are free,
Eternal joy, our destiny.

Embracing the Divine Promise

In shadows cast, your light breaks through,
A promise kept, forever true.
With arms outstretched, we seek your grace,
In every heart, your warm embrace.

Ascend with us, O mighty Lord,
In trials faced, your love's our sword.
With every challenge, strength we find,
In every moment, hearts aligned.

The divine promise, strong and bright,
Guides us along through darkest night.
In unity, we stand as one,
Embracing faith, our journey's begun.

In whispers soft, your spirit calls,
Across the ages, your love enthralls.
In every life, your touch remains,
In loving bonds, your truth sustains.

So let us walk, with courage bold,
Embracing promises of old.
In faith and love, we rise and sing,
Eternal joy, our offering.

Energy of Healing

In stillness, grace descends,
Soft whispers mend the hearts,
Light entwines each wounded soul,
Divine love never parts.

Hands uplifted, we invoke,
The balm of faith in prayer,
Unity brings forth the light,
In sacred breath we share.

From shadows we arise anew,
Cleansed by rivers of hope,
Restoration in His arms,
Together we will cope.

Each heartbeat sings His name,
A melody profound,
In the energy of healing,
Divine connections found.

Let us walk this path of peace,
A journey hand in hand,
For in every act of love,
We find His perfect plan.

A Covenant of Wholeness

In sacred union we abide,
Together woven strong,
Promises of love and grace,
In harmony, we belong.

A testament of faith unfolds,
Each spirit intertwined,
In the quiet, whispers rise,
A bond that is divine.

Through trials and through joy,
We gather as one voice,
In the covenant of wholeness,
In Him, we rejoice.

Every tear is understood,
In compassion's warm embrace,
Life's tapestry is richer,
Each thread, a sacred space.

Together in this journey,
With hearts united, free,
We honor every heartbeat,
In divine harmony.

Rivers of Rebirth

Beneath the heavens' watchful gaze,
Our spirits rise and flow,
With faith, we dive in waters deep,
To feel the rivers grow.

In baptism of the morning mist,
Transformation takes its course,
Renewed through trials past endured,
We find our inner source.

With every wave, we shed our pain,
Forgiveness is our guide,
In the currents of our lives,
We gather strength inside.

From ashes we shall soar again,
As dawn paints skies anew,
Through rivers of rebirth,
His promise stays true.

Let joy be our companion,
As we embrace His grace,
For in the flow of spirit,
We find our rightful place.

The Gift of Reconciliation

In shadows deep, we seek the light,
Where hearts can mend and heal,
Through paths of grace, we find our way,
In love, we feel, we kneel.

The gift of reconciliation,
Is precious, pure, and rare,
With open hands, we share our truth,
A sacred space laid bare.

Together on this journey,
We lift each other high,
Through storms and trials faced in faith,
We dare to dream, to fly.

Forgiveness blooms where love abounds,
As prayers ascend the sky,
In the gift of reconciliation,
We live, we learn, we try.

So let us dance in gentle light,
In a circle, strong and free,
For in each heart, the spark ignites,
A shared divinity.

Embracing the Unseen

In shadows deep, the spirit sighs,
Whispers of grace fill the quiet skies.
Trust in the path the heart can't see,
For the unseen realm holds eternity.

Faith like a river flows through the night,
Guiding the lost with divine light.
Each tear and struggle forms sacred art,
Crafting the journey of a faithful heart.

In silence, the soul learns to believe,
With every heartbeat, it learns to weave.
Threads of hope in a tapestry rare,
Embracing the unseen, a divine affair.

Ascend the heights, where visions embrace,
In stillness, the mind finds its place.
The divine whispers through every fear,
Embracing the unseen, our spirits near.

Lift up your gaze to the stars above,
Each twinkle a promise, a sign of love.
Trust in the journey, through thick and thin,
For the unseen grace is where life begins.

Lighthouses of Love

Through tempest waves and storms that roar,
The heart finds safety on love's distant shore.
In each soft glow, a beacon shines,
Drawing us close, entwined like vines.

Lighthouses stand on the rocks of despair,
Guiding lost souls with tender care.
In darkest nights, their light prevails,
Whispers of love fill the silent tales.

Hands held steady, in unity we rise,
Reflecting the light from the warmest skies.
Each candle ignites with a sacred fire,
Stirring the spirit, awakening desire.

In every embrace, divinity dwells,
In laughter and tears, the heart's sweet spells.
Lighthouses gleam with a love so pure,
In their warm glow, our hearts endure.

Together we journey, through calm and strife,
Lighthouses of love illuminate life.
With faith as our anchor and hope as our sail,
In love's embrace, we shall never pale.

The Sacred Reawakening

In stillness of twilight, the spirit awakes,
From slumber so profound, the heart gently shakes.
A whisper of dawn through a veil of dreams,
Brings forth the sacred, or so it seems.

Nature's soft murmur sings out a hymn,
Awakening souls to the possibility within.
In every petal, in every breeze,
Lies the call of the sacred, urging to seize.

Mountains stand tall with stories untold,
In their quiet majesty, wisdom unfolds.
The sacred reawakens in each passing day,
Inviting humanity to find its way.

Each raindrop falling carries a prayer,
For embers of hope in hearts unaware.
As light breaks forth, our spirits align,
In the sacred reawakening, love divine.

So heed the call of the universe wide,
In silence and stillness, let faith be your guide.
In the dance of existence, we find the tune,
The sacred reawakening beneath the moon.

Blossoms of Faith

Amidst the thorns, a flower blooms,
Bringing forth light to dispel the glooms.
With petals soft, it whispers a prayer,
In blossoms of faith, love fills the air.

Each seed planted in the soil of hope,
Grows with persistence, learning to cope.
Even in darkness, it seeks for the sun,
In blossoms of faith, all will be won.

The colors vibrant, a canvas of grace,
Each hue a reminder of love’s embrace.
Through trials and tears, the spirit will grow,
In blossoms of faith, seeds of joy sow.

Gather the petals, share them around,
For in giving and love, true beauty is found.
Together we'll nurture this garden divine,
In the blossoms of faith, our hearts intertwine.

So let us rejoice in the journey we tread,
With courage and love, our spirits are fed.
In every blossom, a story anew,
In the garden of faith, we find our truth.

A Symphony of Renewal

In the stillness of dawn's glow,
Whispers of hope begin to flow.
Every heart in silence prays,
Longing for brighter days.

Beneath the sky, the spirit sings,
Of grace and joy that morning brings.
With each breath, a fresh start blooms,
Chasing away the night's dark glooms.

Winds of faith gently caress,
Filling souls with tenderness.
Renewal arises from within,
A new chapter to begin.

Hands uplifted, voices raised,
In worship, the heart is praised.
In unity, we find our way,
Guided by love's divine sway.

A symphony in every heart,
Melodies of grace impart.
Through trials, we find our song,
In this new dawn, we belong.

Songs of the Redeemed

From ashes rise the voices clear,
Singing songs that all can hear.
Chains are broken, spirits free,
In grace, we claim our victory.

Through darkest nights, the light does shine,
In love's embrace, we intertwine.
While shadows linger, faith stands tall,
Together, we shall never fall.

The journey marked with twists and turns,
In every heart, a fire burns.
In trials faced, we find our way,
Redeemed, we rise to greet the day.

With grateful hearts, we share our song,
In harmony, we all belong.
The hands of grace hold us tight,
Guiding us through darkest night.

Let every tear become a tune,
A testament beneath the moon.
The songs we sing will never cease,
In every note, we find our peace.

The Dance of New Life

In the garden where hopes ignite,
New life dances in the light.
Every petal, soft and bright,
Whispers joy, pure and right.

Embracing blessings, spirits soar,
The rhythm of love we can't ignore.
In every heartbeat, faith takes flight,
Joined in harmony, day and night.

The beauty of creation sings,
An offering of all good things.
In the stillness, we find our grace,
In every moment, a sacred space.

Through trials faced, we weave our tale,
Together, we shall never fail.
With open arms and hearts so true,
We embrace the dance, both old and new.

A circle spun in love's own name,
In the depth of joy, we claim our aim.
With every step, the world we share,
In the dance of life, we find our prayer.

Reaching for the Infinite

In the vastness of the skies,
We find hope that never dies.
With outstretched hands, we seek the light,
In the shadows, we ignite.

Every prayer a gentle plea,
Yearning for eternity.
With each breath, the spirit flows,
In the journey, love yet grows.

Mountains high and valleys deep,
The promise of faith we keep.
Through the storms, we hold our ground,
In the silence, grace is found.

Reaching forth, our hearts aligned,
In the bonds of love, we find.
With eyes set on the stars above,
We walk in faith, we walk in love.

In the dance of time, we rise,
With every moment, reach for the skies.
In the infinite, we find our home,
In love's embrace, we are never alone.

The Heart Tree

In sacred grove the heart does grow,
With branches wide, in love it glows.
Roots entwined in whispers deep,
The promise of the soul to keep.

Each leaf that falls a prayerlet sent,
To skies above, in peace, content.
The gentle breeze, a soft embrace,
In unity, we find our place.

Seasons change, the tree stands tall,
Through storms and sun, it sees it all.
In every shade, in every grain,
A testament to joy and pain.

O heart tree, guide us in our plight,
When shadows fall and dims the light.
With every heartbeat, we are one,
In symphony until we're done.

The Veil of New Horizons

Beyond the mist, where silence speaks,
A new dawn breaks; the spirit seeks.
With every step on sacred ground,
In the unseen, true hope is found.

The veil lifted, the path is clear,
Through trials faced, we cast out fear.
In whispered dreams, the future's bright,
Guided gently by the light.

In every heartbeat, a world reborn,
From ashes dark, new life is sworn.
With open hearts, we gaze ahead,
To horizons wide, where love is spread.

So let us walk with essence pure,
In unity, the spirit's cure.
Through new horizons, hand in hand,
Together we'll make our stand.

Shadows to Light

In the valley where shadows blend,
Hope emerges, our hearts transcend.
Each darkened thought, a veil it seems,
Yet light will break through all our dreams.

As dawn arises, shadows flee,
In light's embrace, we find the key.
With every struggle, strength we gain,
From heartache's hold, we break the chain.

The journey long, yet grace bestowed,
Through faith and trust, our spirits flowed.
In unity, we rise anew,
From shadows dark to skies of blue.

So let us sing, with voices clear,
In every moment, love draws near.
In shadows turned to radiant might,
We are reborn into the light.

Call of the Infinite

Whispers echo on winds of change,
Infinite love, both vast and strange.
The cosmos sings in sacred tones,
A dance of stars, the truth it hones.

In silence deep, the heart can hear,
The call of life, so pure and clear.
Each heartbeat is a sacred breath,
In life and death, we find our depth.

With open souls, we reach anew,
To skies that hold a deeper hue.
Embrace the vastness, seek the grace,
In unity, we find our place.

In every note, in every prayer,
The infinite calls; we are aware.
Together we rise, hand in hand,
In the great pulse of this divine land.

Rebirth in Spirit

From darkness deep, a whisper stirs,
The heart ignites, as faith concurs.
In silent prayer, the soul ascends,
Awakening light, where hope transcends.

Within the depths, a seed is sown,
A spirit born, no longer alone.
With every breath, a new chance blooms,
In boundless grace, despair consumes.

Through trials faced, strength is found,
In sacred trust, we're tightly bound.
With every tear, the past releases,
And joy emerges, the spirit increases.

The journey flows, a river wide,
As love's embrace becomes our guide.
In gentle whispers, wisdom roams,
As we return to our true homes.

Each moment lived, a gift divine,
In light we walk, our spirits shine.
Rebirth indeed, in every heart,
A masterpiece, a holy art.

From Ashes to Anew

In the fire, a spirit breaks,
From ancient trials, the heart awakes.
In shattered dreams, rebirth begins,
New wings unfold where hope now spins.

From ashes gray, a phoenix soars,
Beyond despair, the spirit roars.
With strength renewed, we rise again,
In love's embrace, we find our zen.

The darkened path, now lighted bright,
In unity, we reignite.
A tapestry of souls entwined,
In faith and grace, our peace defined.

Through turbulent storms, we grasp the hand,
Of gentle mercy, our sacred land.
With each heartbeat, resurrection sings,
From ashes rise; the spirit clings.

O wondrous change, the dawn anew,
In harmony, our spirits grew.
Renewed in love, our purpose clear,
From ashes bright, we persevere.

The Light that Heals

In shadows deep, a flicker glows,
The heart's soft whisper gently flows.
A guiding star in darkest night,
The light that heals, it shines so bright.

From wounds once deep, a balm divine,
In every heart, the love aligns.
As spirit lifts and burdens cease,
In sacred peace, we find release.

Through trials borne, the light breaks forth,
In every soul, we find our worth.
With hands outstretched, we heal the pain,
In unity, our love shall reign.

As dawn unfolds, the world awakes,
In every heart, a choice it makes.
To shine and share, to lift the veil,
The light that heals will never fail.

O radiant grace, we stand aligned,
In love's embrace, our hearts combined.
With every step, we shall reveal,
The wondrous truth that light can heal.

Echoes of Redemption

In distant dawns, the echoes call,
Of every heart, of one and all.
Through silence deep, the whispers flow,
In redemption's song, our spirits grow.

With every sin, a lesson learned,
Through trials fire, our hearts have burned.
Yet mercy comes, like gentle rain,
In every drop, the love we gain.

From shadows cast, the light breaks free,
In every soul, a legacy.
Forgiveness blooms, like flowers wild,
In grace restored, we're reconciled.

The past held close, but futures bright,
In hope we walk, hand in light.
For every tear, a promise made,
In echoes sweet, our fears will fade.

O journeys long, we now embrace,
In every step, we seek His grace.
With open hearts, redemption's key,
In love we stand, eternally.

The Bridge to Healing

Upon the waters, calm and still,
A bridge of grace, a sacred will.
Step forth in faith, let spirits mend,
In love's embrace, our souls ascend.

Wounds of the past shall fade away,
As light breaks through the darkest day.
With every tear, a lesson learned,
In quiet strength, our hearts are turned.

The path is long; the journey true,
With hope ignited, we renew.
Find solace here, in gentle hands,
Together, we rise upon Love's sands.

In whispers soft, the healing flows,
A promise held where mercy grows.
Each heartbeat sings a sacred song,
In unity, we all belong.

So let us walk this bridge of light,
With faith that guides us through the night.
The dawn will break; the shadows flee,
For in His name, we shall be free.

Rays of Divine Love

In morning's glow, the sun appears,
A gift of hope, dispelling fears.
Each ray that breaks upon the land,
Is love's embrace, a guiding hand.

With open hearts, we share the light,
A beacon bright, in darkest night.
Together, we shall lift our praise,
In grateful song, through all our days.

For every soul, a spark divine,
In every heart, His light shall shine.
With every breath, our spirits rise,
Reflecting grace from sacred skies.

In unity, we stand as one,
Beneath the warmth of love's sweet sun.
The rays of hope, forever flow,
In every heart, let kindness grow.

So let us walk, hand in hand,
Guided by stars, a promised land.
Together, in this life we weave,
In divine love, we shall believe.

Reflections of Forgiveness

In the stillness of the night,
Hearts awaken, seeking light.
Forgiveness whispers, soft and clear,
A balm for wounds held far too near.

Each shadow cast, a chance to grow,
In mercy's grace, the spirit flows.
Let go the past, release the pain,
In love's embrace, we rise again.

A mirror held to every soul,
In brokenness, we become whole.
With open arms, we let it be,
In unity, we find the key.

Forgive the trespasses we've known,
In every heart, compassion sown.
The chains of anger slowly break,
As love's sweet song begins to wake.

So let us tread a path of peace,
In every heart, let kindness cease.
In timeless grace, we shall abide,
With open hearts, forgiveness wide.

The Resurrection of the Spirit

From ashes rise, the spirit free,
In light reborn, eternity.
With every breath, new life we gain,
In faith's embrace, we break the chain.

The darkest hour must meet the dawn,
In trials faced, we carry on.
With hope restored, the heart shall soar,
In love's vast light, we are reborn.

Let joy resound, our spirits sing,
In every heart, the promise spring.
From sorrow's depths, we find our way,
To brighter shores, where hearts shall play.

In moments lush, we feel His grace,
In every tear, a sacred place.
To rise anew, to find our soul,
In unity, we all are whole.

So let us dance, with spirits bright,
In every shadow, find the light.
For in His love, we shall persist,
The resurrection, our true bliss.

The Quiet Joy of Transformation

In stillness, the heart will bloom,
Where shadows once danced in gloom.
A whisper stirs the soul's delight,
Guiding us toward the light.

With every tear, a seed is sown,
In soil of faith, a life is grown.
The past, a canvas erased and bare,
The Spirit's brush paints with care.

As dawn breaks softly on the hill,
We find within a gentle thrill.
Through trials faced, we come to know,
The quiet joy that ever flows.

In tender grace, we choose to rise,
With open hearts, we clear the skies.
Each moment turned to sacred space,
Transforms the world with love’s embrace.

So let us walk, hand in hand,
In the glow of a promise so grand.
For in our spirits, truth will shine,
Through the quiet joy, divine.

Windows of Grace in the Night

When darkness falls, our spirits soar,
For through the night, there shines a door.
A window open to the divine,
Where love and hope endlessly twine.

Stars emerge in the quiet sphere,
Each twinkle a prayer, sincere.
With every breath, we seek the glow,
Of grace that guides us, ever flow.

In solitude, we find our voice,
In softness, there lies our choice.
To trust in the light beyond our sight,
To find our strength through the night.

As shadows dance, we lift our hands,
In surrender, the heart understands.
For every trial, a lesson grows,
In windows of grace, our spirit knows.

Let faith be our anchor, steadfast,
In the darkest moments, hold fast.
For the light will come to guide our way,
Through windows of grace, come what may.

Holiness Amidst Struggles

In the fray, our hearts do ache,
Yet in the trials, grace we make.
Each struggle bears a sacred sign,
A glimpse of the divine design.

Though burdens weigh and shadows loom,
In darkest hours, we find our room.
For holiness is carved in pain,
A pathway rich for love's refrain.

With hands uplifted, weary souls,
In His embrace, the spirit consoles.
Through every tear, a river flows,
To cleanse the heart, where peace now grows.

Strength rises from the depths below,
In every storm, our spirits glow.
For in the struggles, faith will rise,
And lead us gently to the skies.

So let our voices join the hymn,
In melodies both loud and dim.
For holiness is found in grace,
Amidst our struggles, we embrace.

Winds of Change and Prayer

The winds of change begin to blow,
Whispering truths we need to know.
In every gust, a call to rise,
To dance beneath the open skies.

Through prayer, we find the strength to bend,
With open hearts, our spirits mend.
For in the silence, we discern,
The sacred fire of love will burn.

As seasons shift, our path may wind,
Yet in the storms, our peace we find.
Each breath a promise, sweet and clear,
In winds of change, we cast out fear.

So let us gather in this space,
To seek His counsel, feel His grace.
For every prayer is like a seed,
That blooms in faith, and meets our need.

With every breeze, our hopes ascend,
In unity, our hearts will mend.
For change is but a sacred call,
In winds of prayer, we rise and fall.

The Journey Back to Light

In shadows deep we wander lost,
The path obscured, the soul embossed.
Yet whispers dance upon the breeze,
Guiding us back, our hearts at ease.

Through valleys dark, our footsteps trace,
Each trial a step towards grace.
With every tear, a chance to grow,
The light will come, the darkness slow.

The sun will rise beyond the night,
Illuminating souls in flight.
With faith as our steadfast guide,
We journey forth, hearts open wide.

A beacon shines, our spirits soar,
The love divine forevermore.
Embrace the warmth, let shadows cease,
In light we find our perfect peace.

Together we ascend the height,
In unity, we claim our right.
Our journey back a sacred call,
To find the light that shines in all.

Embracing the Divine Embrace

In love we find a gentle hold,
A warmth that wraps, a story told.
With hands outstretched, we reach above,
Embracing all, the gift of love.

When trials rise, we seek the light,
In every heart, a spark ignites.
The divine presence ever near,
In whispered prayers, our hope is clear.

Together in this sacred space,
We breathe the essence of His grace.
With grateful hearts, we lift our praise,
In each moment, in every phase.

The dance of spirit, pure and free,
Unveiling truths for all to see.
With faith as our eternal guide,
We turn to Him, our hearts abide.

In every step, a sacred chance,
To share the love, to sing, to dance.
In divine embrace, we stand as one,
Together, brighter than the sun.

A Tapestry of Hope

Threads of faith weave through the night,
Colors vibrant, shining bright.
In every storm, a promise stays,
A tapestry of hopeful rays.

Each challenge faced, a pattern new,
With every struggle, strength imbues.
In darkness, light shall find its way,
A guiding star for every day.

With every stitch, a legacy,
Of love and grace, a harmony.
United hearts, a sacred bond,
In this embrace, we feel beyond.

The weaver’s hand, both firm and kind,
Enfolding souls, the lost we find.
In every thread, a story spun,
Together our journey's just begun.

So let our hearts in joy respond,
To weave a world of love beyond.
With every breath, a chance to write,
Our tapestry, a song of light.

The Song of Restoration

In stillness of the morning light,
Voices rise, a sacred sight.
With every note, our spirits mend,
A song of life that shall not end.

The broken pieces find their place,
Together in His warm embrace.
A melody of hope restored,
In love's direction, hearts adored.

As shadows fade, the music swells,
In every soul, the promise dwells.
With every breath, we tune our hearts,
To sing of grace, the healing starts.

In harmony, we join our voice,
In truth and love, we make our choice.
With every lyric, light awakes,
A song of joy that never breaks.

So let us sing, both loud and clear,
A song of restoration near.
In unity, our hope shall shine,
The sacred song, forever thine.

Pathways of Promise

In shadows deep, a light doth gleam,
Guiding hearts with woven dreams.
Each step unfolds a sacred chance,
To walk in faith, to sing, to dance.

With whispered winds, the spirit calls,
Through winding paths where truth enthralls.
Embrace the journey, hold it tight,
For love will lead us through the night.

The mountain high and valley low,
In every trial, His presence flows.
Through storms of doubt, our souls will rise,
With hope that shines like endless skies.

In unity, we find our grace,
Together seeking Heaven's face.
With open hearts, we’ll share the light,
Transforming shadows into bright.

So walk with courage, hand in hand,
For we are part of His great plan.
Emboldened by the love He shows,
Our pathways bright, wherever flows.

The Soul's Awakening

Awake, arise, the dawn is near,
A whisper soft, a call to hear.
In stillness find your sacred space,
The heart awakens to His grace.

With every breath, the spirit sings,
A melody of sacred things.
In quiet moments, truth bestowed,
The path ahead, divinely showed.

In dreams of night, in light of day,
The soul begins to find its way.
Through trials faced and lessons learned,
A flame ignites, our hearts discerned.

Let go of fear, let love arise,
In faith, we soar, beneath the skies.
The journey deepens, wisdom flows,
Awakening the love that grows.

With every step, a story told,
His gentle hand, a guiding hold.
Embrace the light, embrace the truth,
For in our hearts, lies endless youth.

Grace in the Stillness

In moments hushed, the spirit speaks,
A gentle peace, the heart it seeks.
Amidst the noise, find quiet grace,
In stillness, meet the Holy Face.

The world may rush, but we will stand,
With open hearts, and lifted hands.
In silence, hear His soft refrain,
A promise held in joy and pain.

As rivers flow, our souls connect,
In every moment, love reflects.
Through trials faced, we grow in trust,
In every breath, His love is just.

Within the calm, find strength anew,
In every loss, His grace shines through.
With hearts entwined, we shall endure,
In stillness, love remains secure.

So let us pause, and breathe Him in,
In sacred stillness, we begin.
To gather dreams, to heal the past,
In grace, we find our futures cast.

Wings of Transformation

Like gentle winds, our spirits soar,
Through trials faced, we rise and more.
With every shadow, light breaks through,
In grace, we find our hearts anew.

In moments of despair and doubt,
His love will guide us all about.
With wings of faith, we shall arise,
In every heart, hope never dies.

The chrysalis must break apart,
For beauty blooms from every heart.
Transforming pain into the light,
With spirit bold, we own our flight.

Together we shall tread the sky,
With wings of love, we learn to fly.
In unity, we find the strength,
To greet each day, to go the length.

Awake, O hearts, for time is now,
Embrace the change, here and how.
With every step, a promise made,
In love, the fears of life allayed.

Pearls of Wisdom

In silence speaks the truth divine,
The heart yearns for love's design.
With kindness, share the light bestowed,
Through humble acts, our spirits grow.

The path is paved with gentle grace,
In every soul, a sacred space.
Seek knowledge whispered in the night,
For wisdom guides us to the right.

From trials come the lessons learned,
In every heart, the passion burned.
The pearls of time, they gleam and shine,
A gift of grace, so pure, divine.

As rivers flow from mountain heights,
Wisdom falls like gentle plights.
Embrace the truth, let love unfold,
A treasure trove, more precious than gold.

In every glance, the world reflects,
The whispers of divine intellects.
In unity, we find our place,
In every trial, there is grace.

Foundations of Faith

Build your heart on gentle stone,
Where love abounds, we are not alone.
In every prayer, a seed is sown,
With faith, the path to grace is known.

Through trials faced, and burdens shared,
Our spirits rise when hope is bared.
In every shadow, light will bloom,
Foundations strong, dispelling gloom.

With hands held high, we rise and sing,
Of miracles that faith can bring.
In every moment, trust the way,
For love will guide us day by day.

Let hearts unite in sacred space,
In harmony, we find our place.
With every step and every breath,
In faith, we conquer fear and death.

Together, we can climb the heights,
With strength in God, we face the nights.
The pillars strong, our spirits soar,
In faith, we walk forevermore.

The Compass of Hope

In every heart, a compass lies,
It points us toward the endless skies.
With hope as fuel, our dreams ignite,
As stars align, we find our light.

Through storms we face, and winds that wail,
The compass guides, we shall not fail.
In moments dark, a beacon's glow,
The path ahead, in faith we know.

A journey long, but worth the quest,
With every step, we are truly blessed.
In every struggle, find the grace,
For hope will lead us to embrace.

The heart beats strong with dreams held dear,
In every challenge, shed the fear.
The compass spins, but finds its way,
In endless love, we choose to stay.

With every prayer, our spirits rise,
Guided by faith, we touch the skies.
In unity, we stand and cope,
For love is always the compass of hope.

A Return to Wholeness

In life's embrace, we find our way,
Returning to the light of day.
With broken hearts, we seek to mend,
In love's embrace, we find our friend.

Through valleys low and mountains tall,
The call of grace, it beckons all.
With every step, our fears subside,
In wholeness, we choose love as guide.

The past may haunt, but hope is here,
In every moment, shed the fear.
In unity, we rise anew,
A tapestry of love in view.

The journey long, but worth each mile,
With open hearts, we find our smile.
Let go of pain, embrace the light,
For wholeness blooms in darkest night.

With every bond that heals the soul,
In togetherness, we feel whole.
A return to love, a sacred quest,
In every heart, we find our rest.

Whispers of Grace's Embrace

In the silence, grace descends,
A gentle touch that never ends.
From shadows deep, hope starts to rise,
Illuminating darkened skies.

With every breath, a prayer we make,
In whispered tones, our hearts awake.
The warmth of love, a guiding light,
Unraveling the veil of night.

Together we stand, souls intertwined,
In the embrace, the lost we find.
With every step, the path unfolds,
In sacred stories yet untold.

From humble hearts, gratitude flows,
In kindness shared, our spirit grows.
Each act of love, a holy spark,
Igniting faith, igniting dark.

In whispers soft, we seek the flame,
In every heart, we share the name.
Grace surrounds us, pure and bright,
Leading lost souls into light.

The Resurrection of Spirit

When shadows loom and spirits fade,
In darkness deep, our hope is made.
From ashes rise, our hearts reborn,
In sacred strength, we are adorned.

With every trial, we find our way,
In silent prayer, we learn to stay.
The soul’s ascent, a joyous flight,
Emerging bold from endless night.

Awake, arise, the call is clear,
In every moment, love draws near.
From doubt's despair, we claim our voice,
In faith and grace, we make our choice.

In unity, our spirits soar,
Each wound embraced, we heal once more.
The resurrection sings its song,
In harmony, where we belong.

Awash in light, we find our truth,
The fountain of eternal youth.
In every heart, the Spirit’s glow,
A river of love, forever flow.

Dawn of the Soul's Redemption

As morning breaks, redemption found,
In whispered grace, our hearts unbound.
The dawn arrives with light anew,
In every shadow, hope shines through.

With every breath, we taste the day,
In joy and love, we find our way.
The soul awakens, strain and sigh,
Renewed by faith, we learn to fly.

The trials faced, the burdens borne,
In spirit strong, we have been sworn.
To rise again, to love anew,
In every heart, the light shines true.

From darkness deep, the light breaks through,
A promise held, a bond so true.
In every moment, we are blessed,
In sacred love, our souls find rest.

Dawn paints the sky in hues of hope,
In unity, we learn to cope.
With open arms, the world we greet,
In every heartbeat, grace is sweet.

From Ashes to Radiance

From mountains high to valleys low,
In every heart, a seed will grow.
From ashes scattered, we arise,
In strength and grace, we touch the skies.

With every tear, redemption pours,
In every song, our spirit roars.
The journey long, yet none alone,
In love's embrace, we find our home.

Through trials faced, we learn to stand,
With open hearts, we clasp our hands.
From fragments lost, we seek the whole,
In faith, we mend the wounded soul.

Awake, arise, let courage sing,
In every breath, new life we bring.
From dust to dreams, we run the race,
A testament to love's pure grace.

With radiance bright, we light the way,
In unity, our spirits play.
From ashes to stars, our journey's spun,
In every heart, we're truly one.

Glimmers of Faith

In shadows deep, a light does shine,
A whisper sweet, a touch divine.
Through trials faced, our spirits soar,
In glimmers of faith, we seek for more.

When hope seems lost, and doubts arise,
We lift our hearts to the endless skies.
In every storm, His love remains,
A beacon bright, through all our pains.

With every prayer, a seed we sow,
In gardens of grace, His blessings grow.
Unseen yet felt, His presence near,
In glimmers of faith, we cast out fear.

Through silent nights, when shadows creep,
Our souls in trust, forever keep.
With open hearts, we look above,
In glimmers of faith, we find His love.

So let us walk, in courage bold,
With hearts ablaze, His truth unfold.
For in our hearts, His light will stay,
In glimmers of faith, we find the way.

In the Arms of Mercy

A gentle hand, a soft embrace,
In the arms of mercy, we find our place.
With every tear, He wipes away,
A refuge sweet, where we can stay.

When burdens weigh and hopes are thin,
He lifts us high, and love begins.
In every heart, a whisper true,
In the arms of mercy, He comforts you.

The path may twist, the road may bend,
But in His love, we find a friend.
Through every trial, He holds us tight,
In the arms of mercy, we find the light.

With every breath, His grace surrounds,
In quiet moments, His peace abounds.
Through darkest nights, His warmth we feel,
In the arms of mercy, our wounds will heal.

So let us rest, in trust so deep,
In His embrace, our souls shall leap.
For in His care, we're never lost,
In the arms of mercy, love is the cost.

The Seeds of New Beginnings

In earth so rich, new seeds we plant,
With faith and hope, we dare to chant.
Each little sprout, a life anew,
The seeds of faith, in hearts we strew.

From ashes cold, new blooms arise,
With vibrant hues, they touch the skies.
Through every storm, they stand so tall,
The seeds of new beginnings, won't fall.

In seasons change, we find our way,
With open hearts, we choose to stay.
For in the soil of love, we find,
The seeds of new beginnings, intertwined.

In prayers we offer, a hope so bright,
With hands uplifted, we seek the light.
And from our struggles, growth will spring,
The seeds of new beginnings, life will bring.

So cherish each moment, each breath we take,
For every dawn, new joys await.
In faith we trust, our spirits sing,
The seeds of new beginnings, we shall cling.

Harvesting Grace

In fields of gold, we gather joy,
With hearts of gratitude, we employ.
The bounty rich, His love portrayed,
In moments shared, grace is displayed.

With every prayer, we sow the ground,
In faith, abundance will astound.
Through trials faced and lessons learned,
Harvesting grace, our hearts discerned.

As seasons change, our spirits grow,
In every blessing, His goodness flow.
With hands outstretched, we share the gift,
Harvesting grace, our souls uplift.

In unity we stand, souls entwined,
In love's embrace, our hearts aligned.
For every grain, a story told,
Harvesting grace, in faith we hold.

So come, rejoice in the love we share,
In every breath, His heart laid bare.
For in His light, we find our place,
Harvesting grace, in boundless space.

Wings of Restoration

On broken paths we tread each day,
With faith our guiding star to stay.
Through trials deep, we will arise,
On wings of grace that touch the skies.

In shadows dark, a whisper calls,
A promise made, our spirit thralls.
With every tear, a lesson learned,
In heart's warm glow, our hope is burned.

The storm may rage, the night may fall,
Yet love's embrace will hold us all.
With open hands, we seek anew,
The strength to rise and carry through.

So lift your heart, lift up your gaze,
For in the light, our souls will blaze.
In unity, we find our song,
Together strong, we will belong.

The Light After Despair

In darkest hours, when hope seems lost,
We look to heaven, no matter the cost.
Through tears we find a ray of light,
A beacon shining through the night.

From barren grounds, where sorrow sows,
Emerges grace, as love bestows.
With every dawn, new dreams arise,
We greet the sun, where mercy lies.

The path is steep, yet we move near,
With every step, we cast out fear.
For in our hearts, the truth is clear,
That joy awaits, our souls to cheer.

Together walking, hand in hand,
In this great journey, we understand.
The light within is never dim,
For after despair, we rise and swim.

Sacred Renewal in Quietude

In silent moments, wisdom blooms,
Amidst the chaos, calm consumes.
With quiet breath, we seek the truth,
In sacred stillness, finds our youth.

Each whispered prayer, a gentle plea,
Reveals the love that sets us free.
In nature's arms, we find our peace,
As burdens lift and cravings cease.

In solitude, the soul takes flight,
To realms of grace, where hearts ignite.
The whispers of the universe,
In quietude, we find our verse.

Transformed and whole, we walk the path,
Embracing joy, surrendering wrath.
In every pause, we hear the call,
In sacred renewal, we find our all.

Blossoms in the Desert

Amidst the sands where hope seems bare,
A flower blooms with tender care.
In arid lands, where shadows creep,
Life finds a way, its promise keep.

The sun may scorch, the winds may sigh,
Yet petals reach to touch the sky.
With every root that pushes down,
We stand in faith, without a frown.

In trials faced, we grow and thrive,
Just like the blooms, we too survive.
The desert's song, a hymn of grace,
In every heart, we find our place.

So let us learn from flowers bold,
That beauty lives where hope unfolds.
In every struggle, life’s design,
In blossoms found, God's love will shine.

The Embrace of Eternity

In silence profound, we kneel and pray,
The light of the dawn brings hope our way.
With hearts wide open, we seek the grace,
In the embrace of eternity, we find our place.

A whisper of love fills the sacred air,
A promise of peace beyond all despair.
With faith as our guide, we walk hand in hand,
In the warmth of the spirit, forever we stand.

Through trials we pass, our spirits refined,
In the depths of our souls, true freedom we find.
With courage ignited, we rise from the fall,
Bound by the light—divine love's call.

In silence we gather, entwined as one soul,
With every prayer lifted, we make ourselves whole.
Eternity beckons with arms open wide,
In the embrace of forever, our hearts will abide.

So let us remember this sacred truth,
In the journey of life lies the fountain of youth.
For love never fades, and in faith we remain,
Embraced by divinity, forever we gain.

The Echoing Alleluia

In the chorus of angels, a song takes flight,
An echoing alleluia fills the night.
With voices united, we sing and rejoice,
In harmony's beauty, we make our choice.

The stillness awakens as hearts start to soar,
With faith as our anchor, we seek to explore.
In moments of worship, our spirits align,
In the echoing alleluia, our souls brightly shine.

Through shadows we tread, yet light leads the way,
In trials and sorrows, together we stay.
With every hymn sung, we embrace the grace,
In the echoing alleluia, we find our space.

As dawn gently breaks, painting skies anew,
With love as our guide, we hold to what’s true.
In laughter and tears, in joy and in strife,
The echoing alleluia is the song of our life.

So let every heart, every voice now partake,
In this divine rhythm together we make.
For in every moment, His love we pursue,
In the echoing alleluia, our hearts will be true.

Foundations in Faith

Upon the solid rock, we build our space,
With faith as our foundation, we find our grace.
In trials and storms, unwavering we stand,
With hearts intertwined, we walk hand in hand.

The path may be winding, but we do not fear,
For love lights the way, and faith draws us near.
In whispers of hope, we hear the call,
With foundations in faith, we rise from the fall.

In the whispers of prayer, we seek His face,
In moments of doubt, we find our place.
For in every shadow, His light will break through,
With foundations in faith, we are ever renewed.

As seasons may change, our spirits will grow,
Rooted in truth, our hearts all aglow.
Through every challenge, His promise will stay,
With foundations in faith, we'll never lose our way.

So let us be strong, and boldly proclaim,
For life's sacred journey is more than a game.
In unity anchored, and love as our guide,
With foundations in faith, let our hearts abide.

The Reawakening Call

In the stillness of dawn, a whisper is heard,
A harbinger calling, without any word.
In the depths of our souls, the promise unfolds,
A reawakening call, where faith boldly rolls.

With every new day, the spirit ignites,
In the warmth of the sun, we reach for new heights.
Through valleys of sorrow, through deserts so bare,
We rise with His love, our hearts filled with care.

Each moment a blessing, each breath a new start,
In the tapestry woven, His thread is our heart.
In seasons of waiting, in shadows we dwell,
The reawakening call, a story to tell.

Through the laughter and tears, we find our way home,
An adventure of faith, wherever we roam.
With courage ignited, our spirits enthralled,
In the symphony sacred, the reawakening call.

So listen with gladness, let joy fill the air,
For every creation, His love we declare.
In the echo of ages, His promise will be,
The reawakening call, forever we'll see.

The Garden of Forgiveness

In the quiet glade of heart, we find,
Seeds of sorrow left behind.
With every tear, a bloom does grow,
In forgiveness, love's pure flow.

Amongst the thorns, grace does weave,
A tapestry of those who grieve.
With open arms, the spirit mends,
In the garden, love transcends.

Each whisper soft, a gentle breeze,
Carries prayers upon our knees.
Let the past be washed away,
In this sacred place we pray.

Forgive, oh heart, and let it be,
A song of hope, a melody.
In every shadow, light will gleam,
In the garden, life's sweet dream.

We gather round, a faithful crew,
With hands uplifted, hearts anew.
The garden blooms, the spirit shines,
In forgiveness, love entwines.

Breath of the Soul

In the stillness of the dawn, we call,
The breath of life, resounding all.
With every whisper, hope ignites,
In our hearts, the spirit lights.

Life's ebb and flow, a sacred song,
With every heartbeat, we belong.
In each moment, breathe so deep,
Awake the dreams we dare to keep.

In valleys low and mountains high,
The breath of love, a endless sigh.
Every pulse, a testament,
To the grace of time well spent.

In the rush, we often stray,
Yet peace can find its gentle way.
So pause and inhale the sacred fire,
With breath, our souls require.

In every sigh, a prayer we share,
Touch the divine, a sacred air.
In unity, our spirits soar,
The breath of the soul, forevermore.

The Fabric of Restoration

In the loom of life, we weave and spin,
Threads of hope to mend the sin.
Each color bright, a story told,
In the fabric, love unfolds.

With gentle hands, we stitch the seams,
Together, healing broken dreams.
In the tapestry, scars align,
Each flaw a mark of the divine.

Restoration calls to weary hearts,
A promise whispered, never parts.
Each knot a bond of strength and grace,
In the fabric, find your place.

Through trials faced, and battles fought,
In the beauty, lessons taught.
The threads of life, a sacred thread,
In restoration, hope is spread.

So let us gather, hand in hand,
Weaving love across the land.
In every stitch, a future bright,
The fabric of restoration, our light.

A Kaleidoscope of Grace

In moments bright, our spirits dance,
Like colors twirled in wild romance.
Each hue a blessing, bold and true,
In a kaleidoscope, grace breaks through.

With every glance, a new design,
A glimpse of glory, love divine.
We see reflections of the soul,
In unity, we become whole.

Life's shifting patterns, ever clear,
Through trials faced, we persevere.
In every turn, a lesson learned,
In a kaleidoscope, hearts burn.

Together we weave the light of hope,
Through every challenge, we will cope.
For in our hearts, the colors blend,
A tapestry that knows no end.

In the moments fleeting, cherish grace,
Find beauty in each sacred space.
With open hearts, let love embrace,
Life's kaleidoscope, a holy place.

Wings of the Spirit

On gentle winds, the Spirit soars,
Carrying whispers, through open doors.
In silence, we hear the sacred call,
Awakening hearts, embracing all.

In lofty heights, we find our place,
Guided by love, wrapped in grace.
With every breath, a new beginning,
From depths of sorrow, joy is winning.

Each soul a spark, in the vast expanse,
Dancing in rhythm, a holy dance.
Lifted by faith, we rise above,
Carved in the light of boundless love.

Through trials faced, we shall ascend,
In unity, our spirits mend.
With wings of hope, we take our flight,
Into the embrace of endless light.

The Dance of Divine Healing

In shadows cast by worldly fears,
A healing balm, the soul endears.
Step lightly now, for we are one,
In this sacred dance, under the sun.

In circles drawn, the spirits sway,
Melodies of grace, our hearts obey.
With every twirl, the past released,
In the arms of peace, we find our feast.

Unified, we rise like dawn,
Together strong, where light is drawn.
Breath of the Divine, our source of breath,
In love's embrace, we conquer death.

With every step, new life begins,
Through laughter shared, our souls finds wins.
In the dance of life, we intertwine,
Forever grateful for love divine.

Channels of Renewal

As streams of grace flow from above,
We are the vessels of endless love.
In moments still, transformation flows,
Through humble hearts, the Spirit grows.

With each new dawn, we cleanse our sight,
Letting go of darkness, embracing light.
In unity, we seek to be,
Channels of peace, setting souls free.

In every prayer, our hopes arise,
A tapestry of dreams in the skies.
Renewal comes in whispered prayers,
For every heart, the Spirit cares.

In loving actions, we build anew,
A world transformed, with hearts so true.
With every beat, a purpose clear,
In the embrace of love, we draw near.

The Well of Life

In the stillness, a sacred well,
Where wisdom flows, and stories dwell.
In times of drought, it quenches thirst,
A reservoir of love, forever cursed.

From depths unseen, the waters rise,
Reflecting truth in endless skies.
With every drop, the spirit drinks,
In silence found, the soul unlinks.

To gather round, all who seek light,
Sharing the gifts that banish night.
In unity, we draw from grace,
In the well of life, we find our place.

As ripples spread across the land,
Each heart a wave, an outstretched hand.
In the stillness of the sacred flow,
A boundless love continues to grow.

The Cleansing Rain of Love

Gentle drops fall from the sky,
Washing away sorrow’s sigh.
Hearts open wide, like petals bloom,
In the embrace of love, we find room.

Blessed are the hearts pure and dear,
In rain's soft touch, no space for fear.
Each droplet sings a sacred tune,
Inviting grace, like a fragrant June.

As rivers swell with a holy stream,
We lose ourselves within the dream.
Love’s cleansing touch, a radiant flow,
In the heart’s garden, we sow what we grow.

With every storm, a promise true,
Renewal comes with morning dew.
Hearts drenched in faith receive the light,
Guided by love, through the darkest night.

In unity, we stand as one,
Beneath the shining, warming sun.
The rain of love shall wash the pain,
Transforming all in humble gain.

Embracing the Everlasting You

In silence deep, Your presence speaks,
A whisper soft, my spirit seeks.
Eternal truth like rivers flow,
Teaching love, in depths we grow.

Through trials faced, with hands held tight,
We journey forth, igniting light.
In shadows cast, Your love remains,
Banishing doubts, calming my pains.

Hearts entwined, we rise above,
Together bound by sacred love.
In every breath, a vow renewed,
In every step, we walk with You.

The tapestry of life we weave,
In faith and hope, together believe.
With every heartbeat, I hear Your call,
Embracing You, I stand tall.

Our spirits dance in radiant light,
You are my strength, my guiding sight.
In every moment, forever true,
I find my peace in embracing You.

Whispers of Grace

In the stillness, grace does flow,
Soft as shadows, yet keen to show.
With every breath, a breath of hope,
In grace’s arms, the weary cope.

Whispers brushing against the soul,
Healing parts, making the whole.
In the quiet, love takes flight,
Guiding lost hearts to the light.

Like morning mist upon the ground,
In grace, a sacred truth is found.
Restoration blooms through gentle sighs,
Uplifting hearts to boundless skies.

In laughter shared and tears released,
Whispers of grace, our souls increased.
In gratitude, we find our way,
Embracing grace in every day.

For in life's storms, calmness lingers,
In grace’s hold, we find our fingers.
They weave together a tapestry,
Whispers of grace, eternally free.

The Dawn of Forgiveness

As dawn breaks, light enters in,
Unraveling shackles, freeing the sin.
With open hearts, we start anew,
The dawn of peace in skies so blue.

Forgiveness blooms like morning flower,
Beneath grace's gentle, warming power.
In letting go, the soul takes flight,
Reclaiming joy, embracing light.

Each kind word, a healing balm,
In whispered prayers, find the calm.
The heart unbound, no longer sore,
Forgiveness opens every door.

With every dawn, a chance to mend,
To break the cycle, love will tend.
In unity, we rise from pain,
The dawn of hope through gentle rain.

So let us walk with hearts ablaze,
In the beauty of our changing ways.
For in forgiveness, we find our song,
The dawn of love, where we belong.

Miracles in the Mundane

In the quiet dawn, a whisper sings,
Life's gentle touch in common things.
A leaf that dances in the breeze,
Reminds us of the grace we seize.

In humble bread, a sacred rite,
In every step, the path of light.
A smile exchanged beneath the sun,
In each small act, His love is spun.

The morning dew, a fleeting gift,
Nature's way to gently lift.
In simple joys, His presence glows,
In every heart, His mercy flows.

Beneath the stars, the world awakes,
In silent prayer, the spirit shakes.
The laughter shared, the tears we shed,
In all of life, His grace is spread.

In moments brief, the sacred find,
In every breath, His love entwined.
So pause and see, the miracles near,
In every day, His truth is clear.

Reclaiming the Lost Spirit

In shadows deep, where voices wane,
The spirit waits amidst the pain.
A flicker shines, a hope restored,
In quiet hearts, the love outpoured.

With weary hands and burdens high,
We seek the light beyond the sky.
A prayer, a song, to guide our way,
To find the dawn within the gray.

The ember glows, though dim it seems,
In every tear, the spark redeems.
A gentle touch, a soothing grace,
In troubled times, we find our place.

To rise anew from ashes cold,
To walk in faith and to be bold.
With every step, the spirit thrives,
In unity, the hope survives.

Awake, arise, the time is now,
To reclaim joy, to take a vow.
In hearts entwined, we find our strength,
In sacred love, we go the length.

Lighthouses of Hope

In tempest's grip, the waves do roar,
Yet shining bright, the lighthouses shore.
A beacon calling through the night,
Guiding souls toward the light.

Through darkest storms, the heart must trust,
In faith we stand, our spirits robust.
Each flicker bold, a promise made,
In whispered prayers, our fears will fade.

With every beam, a path revealed,
Hope's gentle touch, our hearts can shield.
In shadows formed, the light breaks through,
A sacred bond that lifts anew.

Together strong, we weather thee,
Through trials faced, what's meant to be.
In every storm, the cove remains,
The lighthouse guides through joy and pains.

The shores will sing of love's embrace,
In every heart, He leaves a trace.
So gather round, let courage flow,
For in His light, we fiercely glow.

Unfurling in the Arms of Grace

In silence sweet, the spirit grows,
As petals open, love bestows.
In gentle whispers, life unfolds,
His tender grasp through storms and golds.

In every tear, a lesson learned,
In humble hearts, the fire burned.
To rise again from ashes gray,
In grace we find our perfect way.

With every heartbeat, peace bestowed,
In faith's embrace, our burdens load.
A journey shared, with all we are,
In every soul, we find the star.

The petals fall, yet roots remain,
In every loss, we break the chain.
In trusting arms, we find the space,
To truly live in arms of grace.

So breathe anew, release the past,
In love's embrace, our spirits cast.
Together we shall rise and sing,
In gratitude, His praise we bring.

Gems of Grace

In the quiet fields of faith,
Lie treasures small and bright,
Each kindness blooms like flowers,
Radiating gentle light.

Through trials faced and burdens borne,
We gather love like sparkling gems,
Each moment steeped in grace,
A gift that never ends.

With every prayer that lifts the heart,
We witness wonder unfold,
In the tapestry of life,
A story of love told.

From hearts that yearn to understand,
Compassion glows within our soul,
In unity, we find our strength,
Together, we are whole.

So cherish every whispered hope,
For grace will lead the way,
In harmony, we walk as one,
And greet each brand new day.

The Light After the Storm

When thunder roars and shadows fall,
And tears stream down like rain,
We seek the light through darkest nights,
A hope that soothes our pain.

With every storm that lashes forth,
A promise shines so bright,
That after trials, dawn will break,
And lead us back to light.

The winds may howl, the waves may crash,
Yet faith will hold us strong,
For in the heart of every storm,
Resilience carries on.

As colors bloom in the aftermath,
The soul begins to rise,
Each moment teaches us to see
The beauty in the skies.

Embrace the path of healing grace,
Let joy and peace adorn,
For every heart that finds its way
Will shine like gold at dawn.

Prayers of Renewal

In the stillness of the morn,
We lift our hearts in prayer,
Each word a seed of hope,
A fragrant breath of air.

With open hands and eager hearts,
We seek a fresh embrace,
For every tear that falls,
Brings strength in love's warm grace.

Renewal flows like rivers deep,
Washing our doubts away,
As faith ignites the embers,
To light our sacred way.

Beneath the canopy of stars,
Our dreams begin to soar,
In unity, we rise as one,
With strength forevermore.

So let us gather, hand in hand,
In every dawn's new light,
For prayers of renewal bring us peace,
And guide us through the night.

A Sanctuary of Hope

In the shelter of the heart,
Hope flourishes and grows,
Like a garden full of light,
Where faith in beauty shows.

Each whispered word of kindness,
Is a lantern in the dark,
Illuminating pathways,
And igniting every spark.

With arms stretched wide in welcome,
We find our common ground,
In the sanctuary of love,
Where grace and peace abound.

In moments shared and stories told,
Our spirits start to blend,
Creating bonds of strength and love,
That time cannot suspend.

So may we cherish every grace,
And nurture hope inside,
For in this sanctuary bright,
Together, we abide.

Light Breaking Through the Veil

In shadows deep, the light does creep,
A whisper soft, where secrets keep.
A dawn unveiled, the hearts do sigh,
With grace descending from on high.

Each ray a promise, bright and bold,
A touch of warmth against the cold.
The veil now lifts, the blinders fall,
To witness love that binds us all.

In prayerful silence, spirits rise,
Awakening truth in open eyes.
The sacred glow, a guiding star,
Reminds us who we really are.

Hope weaves through each weary soul,
In light, we find our blessed goal.
As angels sing, and praises swell,
We walk in peace, and all is well.

Together bound, we seek the sight,
Of everlasting, purest light.
In faith we gather, hand in hand,
Embracing love, a sacred band.

The Gift of Everyday Miracles

In morning rays, the world awakes,
With whispered gifts, the daylight makes.
A smile exchanged, a kindred glance,
Each moment blooms, a sacred dance.

The hum of life, a gentle song,
In every heart, we all belong.
A child's laughter, soft and pure,
In such small things, we find the cure.

The rustle of leaves, the breeze that stirs,
In nature's arms, the spirit purrs.
A quiet moment, a breath of peace,
In everyday grace, our souls release.

From trials faced, our faith grows strong,
Each miracle, where we belong.
The ordinary, wrapped in love,
Reflecting light from realms above.

So let us cherish simple sights,
As blessings cloak our earthly nights.
In gratitude, we share the light,
The gift of life, our pure delight.

Chasing the Dawning Light

As night gives way to new day's grace,
We chase the light, a holy space.
Each step we take, a path of prayer,
With open hearts, we breathe the air.

The colors blend, the sky ignites,
In every corner, hope ignites.
The dawn appears, with promise vast,
A journey forward, free from past.

In every shadow, love's embrace,
A guiding hand in life's fast pace.
We seek the truth in morning's glow,
Each moment shines, as spirits grow.

With joyful spirits, we arise,
To find the magic in the skies.
Together moving, hearts unite,
In chasing dreams, we find the light.

Through trials faced, we learn to soar,
With every step, we seek for more.
In unity, our spirits sing,
To welcome in the light of spring.

The Sacred Dance of Forgiveness

In holy rhythms, hearts entwine,
The dance of grace, a love divine.
With every step, our burdens fall,
In sacred trust, we heed the call.

As whispers echo, pain dissolved,
Through mercy's lens, our souls evolved.
A tender touch, a gentle sigh,
Awakens peace as spirits fly.

In broken bonds, new life we find,
In letting go, our hearts aligned.
Each stride we take, in love's embrace,
Releases chains, allows us space.

The music swells, a sweet refrain,
In forgiving hearts, we break the chain.
With open arms, we share the light,
Together healing in love's sight.

So let us dance through joy and grief,
In every moment, seek relief.
In sacred unity, we strive,
Through the dance of life, we thrive.

Sanctuary in the Storm

In shadows deep, we seek the light,
A refuge found in dark of night.
With faith our shield, and prayer our plea,
We find our strength, so close to Thee.

The winds may howl, the waters rise,
But in Your grace, our spirit flies.
The calm within the raging sea,
Is where our hearts are truly free.

With every trial, we learn to trust,
In You, O Lord, our hearts are just.
Through tempests fierce, we hold Your hand,
A sanctuary, our promised land.

When darkness falls, we'll sing Your praise,
In stormy nights, we find Your ways.
A shelter strong, Your love remains,
In every storm, Your peace sustains.

So lift us high, O Lord above,
In storms of doubt, we feel Your love.
Together, held in faith so warm,
We find our peace, our safe, sweet storm.

Rebirth Through Faith's Fire

In flames of trial, we rise anew,
From ashes past, our spirits grew.
Through heat and pain, we learn to see,
The strength bestowed, O Lord, by Thee.

Our burdens borne, we stand in grace,
Each weary step, a holy trace.
With every watchful, weary sigh,
We find our wings, we learn to fly.

Where shadows fall, a light ignites,
A vision clear, through darkest nights.
In faith's embrace, no fear can reign,
For in Your love, we break the chain.

From sorrow's depth, we seek the shore,
With hearts ablaze, we long for more.
Through storms of doubt, our spirits soar,
In rebirth's fire, we are restored.

So forge in us, O Creator true,
A heart of gold, forever new.
Through trials faced and battles won,
In faith's pure fire, we are reborn.

Celestial Waters Flow

In rivers pure, Your grace does stream,
A flow of love, a holy dream.
With every drop, sweet mercy's gift,
In Celestial waters, souls uplift.

Refresh our hearts, O Lord divine,
In sacred pools, Your light we find.
Through gentle waves, we learn to trust,
In every tide, Your will is just.

The currents guide, the floodgates burst,
In Your embrace, our hearts are nursed.
With every wave, a chance to grow,
In Celestial waters, life will flow.

As storms may rise, and shadows play,
Your waters keep all doubt at bay.
The depths of grace, we now explore,
In living waters, evermore.

So let us wade, O Lord, we pray,
In mercy's tide, we find our way.
With open hearts, we dive and know,
In Celestial waters, love will grow.

The Altar of New Beginnings

At dawn of hope, we gather round,
An altar built on sacred ground.
With hearts laid bare, we offer prayer,
In new beginnings, we lay our care.

In whispered vows, the past we shed,
With every step, new lights ahead.
This altar holds our dreams anew,
O Lord, we trust in all You do.

In love's embrace, we find our way,
Through trials faced, we learn to stay.
Each moment counts, a chance to grow,
At the altar's grace, we overflow.

With hopes ignited, spirits bright,
We seek the dawn, we search for light.
The altar stands, a promise made,
In new beginnings, fears will fade.

So lead us forth, O Lord, we plea,
In faith, we rise, set our hearts free.
Together strong, we walk Your path,
At the altar's heart, we find true math.

In every breath, we feel the call,
To start again, O Lord of all.
At the altar, our hopes take flight,
In new beginnings, we find the light.

Rising Beyond the Shadows

In twilight's embrace, we seek the light,
The path illuminated, dispelling the night.
Faith lifts our spirits, pure and strong,
We rise beyond shadows, where hearts belong.

With every step forward, burdens release,
In the warmth of compassion, we find our peace.
Through valleys of sorrow, we learn to fly,
As the dawn whispers softly, our souls soar high.

Hope leads the way, a beacon aglow,
Guiding the weary, through pain and woe.
In unity's grace, we gather our might,
Together we stand, emerging from night.

With courage ignited, we forge ahead,
In the chant of the faithful, love is widespread.
Each trial a lesson, each tear a prayer,
A testament written in the depths of despair.

So we rise, undaunted, from ashes of doubt,
Mounting the heavens, our spirits shout.
In the arms of the sacred, we find our song,
Forever united, forever strong.

The Garden of Second Chances

In the garden of grace, where souls intertwine,
Blooms of forgiveness, sweet and divine.
Here, wounds can be mended, paths can renew,
As love casts away the shadows it drew.

Every flower whispers of trials once faced,
A tapestry woven with time and with grace.
The soil of our hearts, rich with the past,
In the light of tomorrow, true healing is cast.

Roots intertwining, a promise to stay,
In the embrace of renewal, the old slips away.
Second chances blossom, each petal a prayer,
Nurtured by kindness, our burdens laid bare.

With hands opened wide, we gather the seeds,
Planting our hopes amidst deserts and weeds.
Together we flourish, in harmony's dance,
In the garden of faith, we give life a chance.

So let us rejoice in the love that we share,
In the garden of second chances, we find our care.
A sanctuary sacred, alive with our dreams,
In this haven of healing, forever it gleams.

Sacred Pilgrimage Within

On the journey within, we wander the soul,
Each turn unveils mysteries, plays a role.
With courage to face what the heart tries to hide,
In the silence of stillness, divinity resides.

Steps echo softly on paths ever deep,
In the valleys of spirit, secrets we keep.
With each rising dawn, awareness unfolds,
Revealing the treasures that true faith holds.

Let the mind be the compass, the heart be the guide,
In the sacred pilgrimage, let love abide.
Through shadows and light, we seek and we find,
The whispers of heaven entwined in the mind.

Resilience gathers in moments of prayer,
In the sanctuary sacred, we learn to share.
With every breath taken, we cultivate grace,
As we walk this pilgrimage, we find our place.

So let the world fade, if just for a while,
In the journey within, embrace every mile.
For in seeking the truth, our spirits will soar,
In this sacred pilgrimage, we are evermore.

When Hope Takes Wing

When hope takes wing, the heart understands,
The promise of dawn in the simplest of plans.
With dreams as our feathers, we rise from the ground,
In the embrace of the heavens, our souls dance around.

Through trials that test us, we learn to believe,
In the light of compassion, we each can achieve.
Together we'll soar, unshackled and free,
In the symphony crafted by faith's melody.

With whispers of courage, we lift up our eyes,
Finding strength in the struggle, we reach for the skies.
In the warmth of connection, our spirits align,
As hope takes its flight, every heart will shine.

Aligned with the stars, we craft our own fate,
In the tapestry woven, our dreams resonate.
Hand in hand with tomorrow, we find our way,
When hope takes wing, night gives way to day.

So let the winds carry us, wherever they may,
In the journey of kindness, together we stay.
When hope takes wing, a promise unfolds,
In the hearts of believers, a story is told.

From Doubt to Devotion

In shadows deep, where questions grow,
A flicker sparks, a gentle glow.
From doubts that wrack the weary soul,
To faith that fills and makes one whole.

Through trials faced and burdens borne,
A heart once lost now greets the morn.
With open hands, I lift my plea,
In trust I stand, set free, I see.

Each tear that fell, a seed of grace,
Transformed in light, now shines its face.
With every prayer, the roots go deep,
From doubt to love, my heart shall leap.

In silent whispers, guidance found,
A voice of truth, the lost surround.
In every moment, holy gift,
From doubt to hope, my spirits lift.

So here I stand, in faith renewed,
Embracing light, by love imbued.
A journey shared, where all can see,
From doubt to trust, I long to be.

The Song of Restoration

In brokenness, a sweet refrain,
A melody that heals the pain.
With every note, the past dismissed,
In harmony, I find my bliss.

The weary heart, now beats anew,
In grace, restored, in joy imbued.
Through trials faced, the song takes flight,
A symphony of love and light.

From ashes rise, the spirit strong,
In every breath, a vibrant song.
Each verse a step, toward brighter days,
In faith, I walk, along Your ways.

Together sung, a chorus bright,
In unity, we find our might.
With every heart, the tune expands,
In restoration, we make our stands.

So let us lift our voice in praise,
For every moment, in all our days.
The song of life, forever true,
In restoration, we are made anew.

Threads of Faith Woven Anew

In sacred loom, with threads so fine,
Each heartbeat echoes love divine.
Through trials met, we intertwine,
In faith, we weave, our lives align.

From memories lost, to hopes reborn,
In every stitch, our spirits adorn.
With hands of grace, the fabric grows,
In unity, the love bestows.

With colors bright, each path we take,
In woven strength, we shall not break.
Together strong, in joy we stand,
In threads of faith, we hold each hand.

Through storms we pass, the fabric bends,
Yet faith remains, the love transcends.
With open hearts, we face the dawn,
In woven hope, our fears are gone.

So let us stitch with tender care,
In every prayer, a love to share.
In faith's embrace, we find our due,
In threads of love, we're ever true.

The Harvest of a Grateful Heart

In fields of grace, the harvest blooms,
With grateful hearts, dispelling gloom.
Each blessing gathered, light reflects,
In love's abundance, joy connects.

The seeds of kindness, deeply sown,
In every heart, true love has grown.
With open hands, we gather near,
In gratitude, we shed our fear.

For every trial, a lesson learned,
In faith's embrace, our souls have yearned.
With every thank you, blessings flow,
In grateful hearts, the love we know.

So let us raise our voice in song,
For every moment, where we belong.
In harvest time, we lift our plea,
With grateful hearts, forever free.

In every smile, in every part,
We celebrate a grateful heart.
In love’s embrace, the light we hear,
The harvest blooms, our path is clear.

Milton Keynes UK
Ingram Content Group UK Ltd.
UKHW020040271124
451585UK00012B/954

9 789916 89815